Original Death Rabbit

by Rose Heiney

World stage premiere at Jermyn Street Theatre, London
9 January – 9 February 2019
Press performance Friday 11 January

Original Death Rabbit
by Rose Heiney

CAST

THE ORIGINAL DEATH RABBIT	Kimberley Nixon

CREATIVE TEAM

DIRECTOR	Hannah Joss
DESIGNER	Louie Whitemore
LIGHTING DESIGNER	Adam King
SOUND DESIGNER & COMPOSER	Alexandra Faye Braithwaite
STAGE MANAGER	Caroline Lowe
ASSISTANT DIRECTOR	Kennedy Bloomer
PRODUCTION MANAGER	Will Herman
PRODUCTION PHOTOGRAPHER	Robert Workman

Produced and general managed by Jermyn Street Theatre.

With thanks to St Pancras Old Church, St James's Church, Piccadilly; Esmé Thompson, Alex Pearson, Hannah Lawrence, Sean Ryan, Abi Duddleston at The National and Duncan Fraser.

Cast

KIMBERLEY NIXON | THE ORIGINAL DEATH RABBIT

Theatre includes: *Girl With a Pearl Earring* (Theatre Royal Haymarket). Television includes: *Fresh Meat*, *Ordinary Lies* (Channel 4); *Cranford* (BBC); *Critical* (Sky One). Film includes: *Angus, Thongs and Perfect Snogging*, *Wild Child*, *East Virtue*, *Offender*, *Cherrybomb*. Kimberley Nixon is a BAFTA Award-winning actress.

Creative Team

ROSE HEINEY | WRITER

Theatre includes: *Elephants* (Hampstead); *Come To Where I'm From* (Paines Plough/Chipping Norton). Television includes: *Fresh Meat*, *Big Bad World*, *Miranda*. Books include: *The Days of Judy B* (Short Books). Radio includes: *Home Alone*, *From A–Z*, *From Fact to Fiction*, *Original Death Rabbit* starring Jessie Cave. Rose has television and feature projects in development with Working Title and Moonage Pictures, and is currently writing on the Filmwave/Netflix series *Letter for the King* which is filming currently.

HANNAH JOSS | DIRECTOR

Theatre includes: *Carry On Jaywick* (Murphy&Co); *Eigengrau* (King's Head); *The 11th Hour* (The Egg, Theatre Royal Bath); *That Moment* (Crescent Arts, Belfast). As Associate Director: *Box of Delights* (Wilton's Music Hall); *The Adventure* (Lyric Hammersmith/national tour). As Assistant Director: *Dance Nation* (Almeida); *Woyzeck* (Old Vic); *Revolt. She Said. Revolt Again.* (Royal Shakespeare Company); *Incognito* (HighTide/Bush); *The Teacup Poisoner* (The Egg, Theatre Royal Bath); *The Ladykillers* (Watermill). Hannah is a Resident Director at the Almeida Theatre and was Baylis Assistant at the Old Vic.

LOUIE WHITEMORE | DESIGNER

For Jermyn Street Theatre: *Miss Julie*, *Hound of the Baskervilles*, *Tonight at 8.30*, *Tomorrow at Noon.* Other theatre includes: *Handbagged*, *Single Spies*, *Bold Girls* (Theatre by the Lake/York Theatre Royal); *Stewart Lee: Content Provider* (UK tour); *Blythe Spirit* (Beijing); *Good Soul* (Young Vic); *The Minotaur*, *My Father Odysseus* (Unicorn); *The Winter's Tale* (NAPA Karachi); *Lost Land* (Jenin, Palestine); *Potted Sherlock* (Vaudeville/UK tour); *Three Birds* (Bush/Royal Exchange); *Egusi Soup* (Soho); *Mud* (Gate); *The Dog, the Night and the Knife* (Arcola); *Shakespeare Untold*, *The Magic Playroom* (UK tour/Pleasance); *I am a Superhero* (Old Vic New Voices at Theatre503). Opera includes: *Messiah* (Danish opera/Frankfurt opera); *Carmen* (Dorset Opera); *Banished* (Blackheath Halls); *The Magic Flute*, *Carmen*, *La bohème*, *Albert Herring*, *The Marriage of Figaro* (costume design for CoOpera Co). Dance includes: *Egle* (Lithuania National Ballet); *The Nutcracker* (Shanghai Ballet); *Egle, Angelina Ballerina* (English National Ballet); *Choreographics*, *Dance Journeys* (English National Ballet at Sadler's Wells/The Barbican). Louie is an OldVic12 2016 finalist, JMK 2010 Finalist, was OffWestEnd nominated for Best Set Designer for *Miss Julie* and *Tonight at 8.30* (Jermyn Street Theatre) and OffWestEnd nominated for Best Costume Designer for *The Daughter-in-Law* (Arcola).

ADAM KING | LIGHTING DESIGNER

For Jermyn Street Theatre: *The Wasp.* Other theatre includes: *Peter Pan* (New Theatre Royal); *Aladdin* (Harlow Playhouse); *Brass* (Mountview); *Footloose* (StageCoach); *Beauty and the Beast* (New Theatre Royal); *San Diego*, *Gidea Park* (Jacksons Lane); *Hairspray* (Arts Depot); *The Alchemist* (Nuess, Germany); *Montagu* (Tabard); *Clybourne Park*, *The Alchemist* (Karamel Club); *9 to 5 the Musical, King of Hearts* (Bridewell); *Dog Ends* (Tabard); *The Night Before Christmas* (Luton Library); *Grown Up* (Camden People's Theatre); *Broken Strings*, *A Flea in Her Ear* (Tabard); *Hamlet* (Bussey Building); *HOODS – The Musical* (Bernie Grants Arts Centre); the *Stories Before Bedtime* series (Criterion). Recent dance credits include lighting for Royal Ballet School productions (Royal Opera House/Opera Holland Park). Adam is a Lighting Designer for theatre and ballet based in London. He trained at Mountview Academy of Theatre Arts graduating with a BA (Hons) Degree in Technical Theatre, specialising in Lighting. Adam has recently worked as Assistant Lighting Designer to Neil Austin on the Olivier Award-winning *Harry Potter and the Cursed Child* (Palace) and *Bend It Like Beckham* (Phoenix). Adam's own designs have seen him light in a variety of venues from fringe theatres, to the main stage at the Royal Opera House.

ALEXANDRA FAYE BRAITHWAITE | SOUND DESIGNER & COMPOSER

Theatre includes: *Things of Dry Hours* (Young Vic); *Talking Heads, Rudolph* (Leeds Playhouse); *Acceptance* (Hampstead); *Chicken Soup* (Sheffield Crucible); *Dublin Carol* (The Sherman); *Room* (Stratford East/The Abbey); *When I am Queen* (Almeida); *The Remains of Maisie Duggan* (The Abbey); *Happy to Help, Distance* (Park); *The Tempest* (Royal & Derngate); *Diary of a Madman* (Gate/raverse); *The Rolling Stone, Cougar, Dealing with Clair* (Orange Tree); *The Future* (The Yard); *Juicy & Delicious* (Nuffield).

KENNEDY BLOOMER | ASSISTANT DIRECTOR

Directing credits include: *When It Happens* (Tristan Bates); *Healing Wounds* (Wardown Park House); *Mouth Wide Shut* (Moors Bar); *The Roundheads* (Moseley Old Hall); *Oh No It Isn't* (The Hope); *Broken* (Old Red Lion); *TüManz TüK18* (Leicester Square); *Pareidolia* (Karamel Club). Assistant directing credits include: *There but for the grace of God – (go I)* (Soho/Camden People's Theatre/ARC, Stockton); *Foul Pages* (The Hope); *Thark* (Drayton Arms); *Comedy of Errors* (Karamel Club). Kennedy is also Marketing and Publications Officer at Jermyn Street Theatre.

JERMYN
STREET
THEATRE

Jermyn Street Theatre is celebrating its twenty-fifth birthday in 2019.

During the 1930s, the basement of 16b Jermyn Street – close to Piccadilly in the heart of London's West End – was home to the glamorous Monseigneur Restaurant and Club. The space was converted into a theatre by Howard Jameson and Penny Horner in the early 1990s, and Jermyn Street Theatre staged its first production in August 1994. The theatre director Neil Marcus became the first Artistic Director in 1995 and secured Lottery funding for the venue; the producer Chris Grady also made a major contribution to the theatre's development. In the late 1990s, the Artistic Director was David Babani, later the founder and Artistic Director of the Menier Chocolate Factory.

Over the last twenty-five years, the theatre has established itself as one of London's leading Off-West End studio theatres, with hit productions including *Barefoot in the Park* with Alan Cox and Rachel Pickup, directed by Sally Hughes, and *Helping Harry* with Adrian Lukis and Simon Dutton, directed by Nickolas Grace. Gene David Kirk, accompanied by Associate Director Anthony Biggs, became Artistic Director in the late 2000s and reshaped the theatre's creative output with revivals of rarely performed plays, including Charles Morgan's post-war classic *The River Line*, the UK premiere of Ibsen's first performed play *St John's Night*, and another Ibsen, *Little Eyolf* starring Imogen Stubbs and Doreen Mantle. Tom Littler staged two acclaimed Stephen Sondheim revivals: *Anyone Can Whistle*, starring Issy van Randwyck and Rosalie Craig, and *Saturday Night*, which transferred to the Arts Theatre.

In 2012, Trevor Nunn directed the world premiere of Samuel Beckett's radio play *All That Fall*, starring Eileen Atkins and Michael Gambon. The production subsequently transferred to the Arts Theatre and then to New York's 59E59 Theatre. Jermyn Street Theatre was nominated for the Peter Brook Empty Space Award in 2011 and won The Stage 100 Best Fringe Theatre in 2012. Anthony Biggs became Artistic Director in 2013, combining his love of rediscoveries with a new focus on emerging artists and writers from outside the UK. Revivals included Eugene O'Neill's early American work *The First Man*, Terence Rattigan's first play *First Episode*, John Van Druten's First World War drama *Flowers of the Forest*, and a repertory season of South African drama. New works include US playwright Ruby Rae Spiegel's *Dry Land*, Jonathan Lewis's *A Level Playing Field*, and Sarah Daniels' *Soldiers' Wives* starring Cath Shipton.

In 2017, Jermyn Street Theatre started a bold new chapter, becoming the West End's newest and smallest producing theatre. Under the leadership of Artistic Director and Executive Producer Tom Littler, a small in-house producing team create or co-produce all the theatre's productions. Partnerships have been forged with numerous regional theatres including English Theatre Frankfurt, Guildford Shakespeare Company, the Stephen Joseph Theatre, Theatre by the Lake, Theatre Royal Bath, the Watermill Theatre, and York Theatre Royal.

Jermyn Street Theatre's first two years as a producing theatre have seen five seasons of work: the Escape, Scandal, Reaction, Rebels, and Portrait Seasons. These have included fifteen world premieres, European premieres of American drama, several major rediscoveries, Christmas comedies, and acclaimed new translations of classic plays. The theatre is committed to equal gender representation both onstage and offstage. It is also committed to paying a fair and legal wage, and has a bespoke agreement with the industry union, Equity. A Director's Circle of private donors is key to the theatre's survival and growth.

In 2018, Littler directed the most ambitious project in the theatre's history – the first complete London revival since 1936 of Noël Coward's nine-play cycle *Tonight at 8.30*. Deputy Director Stella Powell-Jones brought *Tomorrow at Noon* to the stage – three contemporary responses to Coward's work by female playwrights. The two productions ran side-by-side leading to thirty-six one-act plays performed each week, with tremendously popular trilogy days on Saturdays and Sundays.

Throughout its history, the theatre's founders, Howard Jameson and Penny Horner, have continued to serve as Chair of the Board and Executive Director respectively, and the generous donors, front-of-house staff, and tireless volunteers all play their parts in the Jermyn Street Theatre story.

SUPPORT THE JERMYN STREET THEATRE

Everybody needs their best friends, and every theatre needs them too. At Jermyn Street Theatre we have recently started a Director's Circle. Limited to twenty-five individuals or couples, these are the people we rely on most. They sponsor productions, fund new initiatives, and support our staff. It is a pleasure to get to know them: we invite Director's Circle members to our exclusive press nights and parties, and we often have informal drinks or suppers in small groups. They are also an invaluable sounding board for me. Currently, members of the Director's Circle donate between £2,000 and £55,000 (with a threshold of £2,000 to join). They are our heroes and they make everything possible. We have space at the table for more, and I would love to hear from you.

Tom Littler
Artistic Director

THE DIRECTOR'S CIRCLE

Anonymous

Michael & Gianni Alen-Buckley

Philip & Christine Carne

Jocelyn Abbey & Tom Carney

Colin Clark

Flora Fraser

Charles Glanville & James Hogan

Marjorie Simonds-Gooding

Peter Soros & Electra Toub

Martin Ward & Frances Card

Robert Westlake & Marit Mohn

Melanie Vere Nicoll

AT JERMYN STREET THEATRE

Find us at www.jermynstreettheatre.co.uk @JSTheatre
Box Office: 020 7287 2875
16b Jermyn Street, London SW1Y 6ST

Jermyn Street Theatre is a charitable trust, Registered Charity No.1019755. It receives no regular statutory or Arts Council funding. Ticket sales account for around two-thirds of the costs of each production, with the remainder met through generous private donations, bequests, trusts and foundations, and corporate sponsorship. Subsidising our overheads and our productions requires around £300,000 each year.

ORIGINAL DEATH RABBIT

a monologue

Rose Heiney

This text went to press before the end of rehearsals and so may differ slightly from the play as performed.

A tiny, very messy studio flat. The mess is pretty dense; we're almost in hoarder territory, but not quite.

On the walls are posters pertaining to the four major Richard Curtis films – Four Weddings and a Funeral, Notting Hill, Love Actually *and* About Time.

And a small shelf of books – old, cloth-and-leather-bound books.

There is a little table and chair set up in the centre of the flat. The bit of wall behind the table is white, and free of posters (this is important as we're going to project things on to it later).

There's a laptop open on the table.

A young woman who believes herself to be an **UGLY CUNT** *– so that's what we'll call her throughout – is sitting on a swivel chair in front of the laptop, staring at the screen.*

She is wearing an old, bright-pink, animal-print fluffy onesie with a hood, which has large fluffy pink-and-white bunny ears on it.

The UGLY CUNT *is using the Photo Booth application on her laptop. Stares very, very seriously at the screen. Adjusts her ears so they are straight. Presses a key, and we hear the one-two-three Photo Booth countdown, then a too-loud sound and a too-bright flash as her selfie (stiff, solemn, fluffy-eared selfie) is projected brieflly on to the wall behind her.*

Webcam working, let's begin.

The UGLY CUNT *addresses the webcam. She speaks with a slight mockney accent.*

It comes and goes. Stronger at the start of the monologue – fades totally away to RP at the end.

She is swigging from a bottle of vodka throughout.

Okay.

You probably know who I am, if you're watching this. Unless it's gone viral, and you're new to this, and you've had to read up. In which case – Hiiiiii!! I'm – you can google my real name, if you're really that desperate to know it. All you need to know is I'm thirty-one years and three-hundred-and-sixty-four days old, I have twenty-eight thousand seven hundred and eighty-seven followers on Twitter. People have opinions about me. I am a tiny but inarguably significant fragment of the internet.

I was a thing, you see. I was a pretty bloody big bloody *thing*. I was briefly – very briefly – a *meme*. A craze. One of the first.

What happened was – okay, hold on – just a minute –

She scrolls through her iPhone picture library.

Aha.

She brings up a picture of the herself, a few years younger – it's projected onto the wall behind her. In the photo she's wearing the same rabbit onesie she's wearing now, over full academic dress. She's with two friends, and they're standing outside the Oxford University Examination Schools, celebrating the end of their Finals. Champagne, party poppers, etc. She looks wild, happy, excited.

June 2006. Twenty-one years old, just finished finals. Got a First, thank you very much – (*Burps, loudly, then curtsies.*) English Literature.

You probably hate me now because I went to Oxford, don't you? You've *turned*. You were inching towards interest, sympathy, blah blah blah but now you're all like 'Elite! Bullingdon! Bullingdon! Incest! Beagles! Die! Die! Pitchfork! Die!' Well FYI that's your problem, not mine. What do you want me to say? 'My old man's a dustman.' Sorry.

Actually, fuck it – I'm going to tell you more about Oxford. And you can all tweet at me what an overprivileged cunt I am, and you'll enjoy that and feel great about yourselves, and I won't know about it, or care any more. So I'll tell the truth. I went to Oxford because I loved poetry. Love loved love loved LOVED the fustiest and most unfashionable poems ev-ah.

When I was twelve, I howled with laughter at Edward Lear,
'The Owl and the Pussycat' – my dad used to read it me and
I thought it was the best and cleverest and loveliest and funniest
and most beautiful thing I'd ever encountered. I was – what
would I call it now? I'd say, 'I was the patriarchy's little bitch.
Head on Daddy's knee, listening to an old white man reading
old white man poems. Brainwashed scum.'

But for me it was heaven.

Pause.

Then I got older, and I realised that there's a poem for every
situation, every feeling that you've ever encountered. EVER.
There's pain in life, and there's the antidote for pain, which
is poetry.

Words were our family religion – Dad taught sixth-form
English, and wrote a teeny tiny column in the local paper. My
mum was his number-one fan. We were a classic little band of
writers who never-quite-wrote. Mad mad love for books and
films, disowned sense of shackled discontent manifesting as
compliant sweetness – and uttter, utter reverence for anyone or
anything *published*. Rubber-stamped by the clever people.

So in the sixth form at school, I started a website.
www.poemsIlove.com. I was going to put a poem up every week,
and write why I loved it. That was it. What was I trying to do?

I *think* I maybe thought that I was going to end up rich like Bill
Gates? I'm not sure quite how. The internet was new-ish – you
said internet, I thought Bill Gates. Made perfect sense to me at the
time. I was going to be an anonymous internet poetry billionaire.

I only ever posted one poem. 'An Arundel Tomb', by Philip
Larkin.

I'll spare you it. Google it. It's the one where he goes to
a church, and sees an entombed couple, and it ends with him
writing about that –

'almost instinct, almost-true.
What will survive of us is love.'

Pause.

Good, huh?

Pause.

Nuh-uh. Not good.

She takes a swig of vodka.

First term, I made friends with this girl, Penny. She was president of the college feminist society and the socialist society *and* the anarchist society who weirdly held completely amazing and extremely organised picnics – and after we first met she googled me, and found Poems I Love, and sent me this *motherfucker* of an email about how badly Philip Larkin treated women, and how he was now proven to be a racist, and how by allying myself with him *publically* – the 'publically' is important here guys, it had never *occurred* to me that I might have a responsiblity to my 'public life' – I was aligning myself with 'forces of great harm'. It went on and on and on – the basic message was 'You might think you're Hufflepuff, but you are *Slytherin*, my friend.'

And I was *horrified*. I took my website down and immediately wrote a lengthy public Facebook apology to – get this – 'all women, everywhere, *throughout history*, for my actions.' Then I locked myself in my room, and cried for twenty-four hours, which Penny said was 'about right, morally' and I could 'let it go now, if I was willing to behave differently and educate myself.' This could be a 'really positive move for me.'

So I pledged to do just that.

I adopted a certain 'personal style' after that, I guess – I can see, looking back, twenty-twenty hindsight and all that, I'd say –

I turned on myself.

(*Mimicking herself.*) 'I was *suuuuuuuuch* a TWAT when I came here! I liked Philip Larkin!!!! I look back and just *shudder* at what I was.'

And every time I said something like that about myself, I'd feel a little… it was like the first time I'd said something, I'd jabbed a blunt knife in my belly and left it there. And every time I repeated if I'd twist the knife again and again and again until

I couldn't remember *not* being in that kind of pain. You have to drink quite a lot to cope with that level of self-abandonment. Or achieve quite a lot, eat, control. (*Pause.*) Google.

Pause.

There was this one phrase I always had the urge to google. 'I said to my soul.' 'I said to my soul.' 'I said to my soul.' And I never knew where it came from or what it meant. But it was like there was this little… mole in me, happy little mole, who said 'I said to my soul…'

But I always stopped myself. Like some part of me was all 'DO NOT GOOGLE THAT.' Weird.

Anyway. Who cares, right? I was allied with the 'good people' now. I was 'progress'. Penny had said 'well done' to me. And thus politically purified by Penny the sanctimonious eighteen-year-old, I was free to think well of myself.

Pause. Vodka.

I sometimes think that at the heart of every rebel is a desperately good little girl or boy, some sort of Victorian child. That desire to please, to be *good* is so powerful, overwhelming, desperate that the only thing some people can do is ditch the whole lot – baby, bathwater, and go *feral*.

She burps.

The bunny. I'd been given the bunny suit by one of my tutors, as a joke, because at Penny's request I'd done this whole optional women's studies and history of feminism paper where I literally wrote five thousand words on how awful I thought Playboy bunnies were and why. And so he got me this – well, bunny suit. (*Shrugs.*) It made me laugh.

Penny didn't think it was funny. She said that it was an example of patriarchy covertly externalising its contempt for a *woman who speaks* – whatever the fuck *that* is – and obviously I apologised to her and to all women everywhere instantly and took it off. But then she left to do her year abroad as Visiting Fellow of being an over-literate preachy twat-face at Yale, so I put it right back on.

She strokes her chest.

I *loved* the bunny. (*Strokes her lovely soft bunny chest.*) Still love
the bunny. Back in '06, I loved the bunny so much that I didn't
take him off for a fortnight. I slept in the bunny, went to the shops
in the bunny, went to the pub in the bunny. Went to the pub quite
a lot, actually. And when I was having one of my freaky little
OCD moments, I'd sit on my bed with my hands in my lap, and
let the little niggly thought-worms have their say, and they'd tell
me that if I *ever* took the bunny off, even just to let myself
breathe in the heat, somebody would come and kill my whole
family and it'd be my fault.

Swig of vodka.

It did not always smell great, I'll tell you that for nothing.

She stops. A little uncomfortable.

I wish I had some fags. I've had to stop smoking since I've
started wearing the bunny full time again. It's made of – (*Reaches
round and awkwardly grabs the label in the back on the bunny
suit.*) yep, I knew but I had to check – equal parts polyester, rayon
and acrylic, untreated, not flame-retardant, NOT SUITABLE
FOR CHILDREN UNDER SIX YEARS OLD. Which – I
googled this, in 2006, because I like to acquaint myself with the
worst-case scenario in all circumstances – will not only blow up
like a bomb if set fire to, but will somehow also melt itself to my
skin like a sausage casing. So. No fags for me.

Pause. She catches her breath.

Where were we? Yeah. Right, July '06, post-university. I'm in the
bunny. I've finished uni, and I still don't take it off. I'm back at
home now, and I've gone a bit weird. Things aren't great at home
– I mean, *really* not great. '*EastEnders* Christmas special during
a ratings dip' level of not-great. 'Food poisoning on an aeroplane
circling over Gatwick in a storm' level of not-great.

Pause. She goes a bit more defensively mockney.

I'm stalling, I'm scared, I don't I don't want to tell you this
because it's hard to talk about, it's an *actual physical mental and
emotional real-life trauma* – but I'm going to tell you, because

one of the *main reasons I exist* is to fight the stigma surrounding mental-health issues, right? So four days after I left university my undiagnosed-schizophrenic father – it's totes easy not to diagnose, I mean *most* people glaze over in front of the Parliament Channel for a few hours every evening, don't they? – anyway he went, as it were, schizo with a Stanley knife and cut one of our cat Lulu's ears off, then he grabbed me and slashed the back of my hand so my blood mingled with the cat's blood –

She holds up her hand to the webcam – there's a scar across it.

– then I punched him which just freaked him out even *more*, and we all think he would have gone for Mum if she hadn't come at him from behind with a potato masher and bashed him unconscious on the kitchen floor.

Pause.

It's really hard to talk about mental-health stuff. It's like the Israel and Palestine of medical chat. See, that, what I just said – already I'm like 'should I have said "schizo"? Is that offensive? And is it giving you a bad impression of schizophrenic people that I told you that story, as most of them aren't violent, even though my dad briefly was?' And – you know what, fuck it –

She scoots over to the sideboard, opens a drawer and pulls out a packet of cigarettes and a lighter.

I go up, we all go up together. (*Lights the fag.*) Anyway yeah where was I – oh yeah – I'm all like, 'should I have included the detail about the potato masher, as that's kind of a silly item and – even though it's the truth – does that detail make you think that I'm making light of a *really difficult issue*?' You have to say it that way, by the way. Eyes to the floor, shake the head. Mental health's a *really difficult issue*. Really *complex* issue.

Then, if you're some kind of lovely metropolitan *Guardian*-reading liberal you'll then say something like 'I just feel so lucky never to have fallen prey to it myself.' Such generosity, to cover the fact that deep down, perhaps not even *that* deep down, you think it must be something they did wrong which made them that way. *Must* be. Something they did wrong which you yourself would *never* do, like eat Pot Noodles or watch telly in the mornings or go on an all-inclusive package holiday to Benidorm.

Yeah. Really difficult issue.

She stubs out her cigarette.

I never got counselling or anything. Not from that day to this. I'd been – well, this other thing had happened. I'd been strolling along one night in Oxford with Penny, eating chips post-pub, as you do – and these girls had driven past me. Not uni girls, townie girls. They'd slowed down as I passed, and one of them shouted.

'Ugly cunt!'

And I'd shouted –

(*Posh voice.*) 'Excuse me?'

Then they'd shouted.

'Ugly posh cunt!' And they'd thrown some what I hope was water out of their car window at my chips, and driven off into the night. And I'd started crying, and I'd looked to Penny for comfort, like you would from a friend. And Penny – Penny who went to *Benenden*, Penny whose father had *five Labradors*, Penny who was a *fully qualified ski instructor* – said:

'Okay, perhaps they could have made different choices in the way that they expressed themselves? But it's likely that level of rage came from an understandable anger at the socioeconomic fragmentation of Oxford and for you to take this personally would be denying their reality? So this is kind of on you now. Be the change.'

And I cried harder and said what the fuck? And she said there was a socialist bookshop near King's Cross she'd take me to, which would explain it to me. And I said thank you for educating me, Penny, and she said no problem. Any time.

So when Dad happened – when that all kicked off, on the actual day, when the police were there and everything – this was all a bit fresh in my mind, heart, whatever. And when a neighbour whose son had thrown himself under a train fifteen years ago came round and sat down next to me in the bush by the pond and put her arm round me and said:

'For God's sake, love, get help for yourself. Put that first. You take care of you.'

– I'd considered it. But then I'd gone inside and looked around and seen the books, the theatre programmes, the AGA, the Farrow and Ball, the dog, and thought – no. *She* deserved help for herself, the neighbour, because she's got a traditional oo-arr Suffolk accent and lives in a bungalow. But me? NO. It would be so – self-indulgent, so *privileged* for me to talk to someone. Shut the fuck up, posh bitch, and – well, we didn't have this word for it then, but if it had happened now I would have said – 'check your privilege.'

Anyway. Didn't want to talk about it. Fucking embarrassing, to develop schizophrenia in your mid-fifties. Like going to ballet school at thirty-five.

So I just said thank you to the neighbour, then after she left I phoned the vet to find out whether or not I needed to worry about being cut with the knife that had just cut the cat – surprisingly, no! – and cracked on.

Pause.

I wonder if I might not be in this situation now if I'd talked to someone then.

Pause.

The mole popped up that day. The mole in me. 'I said to my soul, I said to my soul.' Whatever the fuck that meant. I ignored him, too.

Pause. Shrug.

Meh! Whevs. Coulda woulda shoulda.

She drinks some vodka.

ON WITH MY STORY! Two days after, I was having a row with my sister. She was all like 'We're all they have. We have to stay here and be here for Mum as a family.' And I was all like

'"*Be here for Mum as a family?*" Someone's been watching too much *Hollyoaks*.' And my sister took exception to this and was all like 'Fine! Fine! Just fuck off back to *uni*' – my sister didn't go to uni because she's slightly the odd one out of our little book-family and it literally once took her fifteen minutes to read the back of a bag of pasta – 'just fuck off back to uni in your stupid *hilarious* rabbit suit!' And I was like 'Fine! *Fine!*' Doorslam, hair-flick, drama. And just to prove I was serious I put the rabbit on and stormed back through the kitchen and headed on out for a motherfucking walk.

Half an hour later. I was romping along and I saw this beautiful old Anglo-Saxon church. It was just heartbreaking – to me, anyway, because me and my family used to go on these long sponsored bike rides, every year, the Suffolk Historic Churches Bike Ride, and this was absolutely the kind of church we'd stop at and and have orange squash and biscuits. I felt overwhelmed so I sat down in the churchyard, leaned back against a gravestone and had a little – well, no, actually – had quite a massive cry. And then – okay, I should have left at this point, but I was really crying so I kind of couldn't stand up – this funeral arrived. The works. Hearse, mourners, all in black, mega-formal funeral. And me, twenty feet away, sitting on the floor in a big pink bunny costume, doubled over and crying. A couple of people glared, as if I was there on purpose. As if I was doing this for fun.

I felt ashamed. I didn't leave – standing up would only have made it worse – so I doubled over and hid my face in my lap and I thought I'd just wait there, tucked behind the not-quite-big-enough gravestone until they went away. I peeped through the cracks between my fingers like a child, and saw a coffin, white coffin – which I judged, incidentally, because who the fuck do you think you are? Elvis? God I was lovely. Anyway – and I saw the mourners. A lot of young men in cheap suits with stunned-mullet faces. Sixteen, seventeen, too young to be wearing suits. I felt bad for them. I felt bad for the funeral. Clearly it was a particularly shit sort of funeral, you know? Young-person funeral. I didn't want to fuck it up for them. I had sympathy.

I stuffed my face back in my hands, and waited. I heard a click, slightly shutter-click-sounding I suppose, then some more, but never imagined a camera, because who takes photos at a funeral? Then when they'd gone into the church I went back to it. Back through the village, back home, back to it all.

She looks away from the webcam. Swig of vodka.

Next day. Front page of the *East Anglian Daily Times*. Big photo, half-page photo of a sweet, smiling boy and the caption 'Brave Wilsons Mourn Brave Jake.' Jake was fifteen, a keen football player whose ambition had been to play for Ipswich Town. He was dicking around by the reservoir with his friends, he'd seen a five-year-old girl fall off a dinghy she was sailing with her dad, and he'd jumped in after her. Never got near the girl – she was fine, her dad got her – but he drowned. The paper called him a 'hero'. (*Pause.*) Really 'attempted hero' would have been nearer the mark, but hey. Local papers love a hero. Hence the funeral photographer; mawkish sentimentality plus prurient grief-tourism dressed up as respect. Nice.

Anyway. Page two, photo of the funeral, and there I was. A dot in the background, unmistakeable pink dot in a sea of black and grey. Gave me a bit of a fright, but… (*Shrugs.*) Whatever. Could have been worse. My face wasn't visible.

Next day. Email from my uni housemate Penny. 'Did the rabbit go to a random funeral??!?!?!' I was scared. Felt like I was in trouble.

'Don't know what you're on about.'

'Check – ' and she named the site. It was one of the first big user-generated stuff-sharing site. It's still going, still the same, only bigger. There's a front page, where whatever 'the big thing' is that week is posted, and some article, then a few other articles in descending order of popularity. Fun stuff, trends, random shit which you'd call 'wacky' if you were from twenty years ago, now you'd just call it – I don't know, shrug, random, whatevs. And then acres and acres of forums – forums beyond imagining. Boundless chat. See, today, the front page is –

(*Pulls up a website on her computer.*) yeah, typical. A four-minute video called 'My Drunk Wife Makes Grilled Cheeses' – two thousand, six hundred and seventy-two comments. Snide thing about how many times Jehovah's Witnesses have incorrectly predicted the end of the world, three thousand, four hundred and fifty-seven comments. A cat appearing to totally check itself out in a hand mirror – over twelve thousand comments. And a bit of 'news' about Edward Snowden – is he still alive? (*Looks up from the screen.*) – God, everyone on here *loves* Snowden. Still! There was this forum thread four years ago 'GIRLS: what sex-things would you let Edward Snowden do to, at or on you right now?' Pretty much everyone said they'd give him a blowjob at the very least, and at some point someone posted 'blowjob for freedom of information!' which got abbreviated to just 'blowjob for freedom', and it kind of became a thing – like, everyone would sign off with it – 'BJFF'. Then the thread kind of petered out, but the meme got resurrected when someone wrote 'freedom' on another thread about illegal file-sharing and someone else replied 'blowjob' for a joke. And the poster was like 'What the fuck? Blowjob?' And some other posters thought that was funny so literally every time someone wrote the word 'freedom' they'd post a comment underneath which just said 'blowjob'. Which some people took massive offence at when there was a thread about Israel and Palestine, because should a conflict in which *little children have died* really be conflated with low sex-humour? Mm? But people kept on posting 'blowjob' any time someone posted 'freedom'. So eventually people just stopped using the word 'freedom', and then somebody said that that was censorship and then it all *really* kicked off. Dramarama.

I don't post in forums any more.

She takes a swig of vodka.

Except my Richard Curtis Film Fan Forum, obviously. Still exists! My filthy little upper-middle heteronormative old-white-man-loving secret. I'm the chief moderator, and I am *totally* in charge. I own the domain name. I built the forums. I choose which threads live, which threads die. I banish trolls. I am the Creator, Mother, Empress, of richardcurtisfilmfamforums.com.

I run a tight ship. My rules are my motherfucking rules and you will abide by them or you will be terminated. They are as follows.

One: We only the discuss the FOUR MAJOR CANONICAL Richard Curtis-authoured romantic comedies. So, *Four Weddings and a Funeral*, *Notting Hill*, *Love Actually* and *About Time*. Anyone attempting to start a forum thread about *The Boat That Rocked*, will be blocked. It is not a proper romantic comedy. Anyone who attempts to start a thread about *The Boat That Rocked* and who also mistakenly refers to it as *The Boat* Which *Rocked*, will be blocked after being sent a brief, mildly abusive message. Similarly, anyone who puts a comma between the words '*Love*' and '*Actually*' will be blocked, unless they can prove that they've got a fucking good reason for having made the mistake i.e. being dyslexic, or loving the film so much that they briefly lost control of themselves. Only-Richard-Curtis-film-positive posts are permitted. My forum is a happy, safe place for those who share enthusiasm for these works to meet and mingle. No snidery, snark, hate, class warfare or doubts about the ultimate triumph of friendship, jollity, jokes and love are permitted.

AND –

Only people who are absolutely genuinely *serious* may post in the forum section 'Just A Girl Standing In Front Of A Boy Asking Him To Love Her' where Richard Curtis Film Fans can ask one another on dates, express romantic feelings, make plans to meet up in real life to watch the films, et cetera et cetera.

So. That's the only forum I still post on. It's the only nice one. You should join. You stick to the rules, and you'll be welcome.

I've digressed. July, 2006. My photo – me in the rabbit at the funeral –

She pulls up the photo and we see it projected onto the wall behind her – it's quite striking. Black-clad mourners, and a huge person-sized pink bunny curled up by a grave in the background, looking as if it's having a nervous breakdown.

– was huge on the site. Huge. Then it went mainstream – ordinary people, non-geek people, started emailing it to each other. It got in the free paper they give out on the London Underground, then it got in the *Daily Mail*. 'Who's the bunny?' By which point people had started to mimic it – they'd sneak into the background of – you know – red-letter settings, often solemn or formal or something, in a big pink bunny costume and they'd curl up in a little devastated ball, and someone would take a photgraph. It was called 'Death Rabbiting'. Like… like planking, or the Harlem Shake, or the thing where you push your cat's face through a slice of bread. Some of them were anodyne, obviously staged things. You know – bunny in the boardroom. Bunny not enjoying Christmas dinner. Bunny at the football. And some of them were pretty bleak – Bunny at the funeral home, next to Granddad's open casket. Bunny at the hospital. Bunny all alone.

She searches her computer for another photograph.

The one which changed it all was 'Bunny At The War Memorial'. War memorial in a small town, somewhere in the midlands. Group of local lads decided to Death Rabbit on the eleventh of November, when some veterans were laying wreaths.

She finds the photograph and it's projected onto the wall behind her. It's a classic Death Rabbiting – ridiculous, devastated doubled-over rabbit photobombing a sad, solemn little service.

It was too much. It was just timing, I think. There'd been a big war memorial vandalism thing up in York – some ruined old hippie on meth had tried to write 'PEACE' on a concrete poppy with his own shit – a week later some bored journo at the *Mail* picked up on 'Rabbit At The War Memorial' and – BOOM! Outrage. State of folk today. Dehumanising effect of the internet. Apocalypse now. This was all *new*, remember. There wasn't Buzzfeed. We still had Ceefax. We were babies.

Two months later. I'd just stepped out of the valley of screaming ghosts aka my family home, moved to London, shared flat in Hackney, and they found me. Fuck knows how. Guy on the doorstep, six in the morning like he was a bailiff. Asked for a comment. 'Just like to get your side of the story, as the Original Death Rabbit.' I just stood on the doorstep of my shit flat crying and saying sorry sorry sorry sorry sorry as if I'd actually done something wrong, as if I'd actually *solicited* this, and someone

took a photograph and put it in the paper the next day, and
the stuff-sharing site, the same site which kicked it all off,
up the photo, someone wrote a snide little article underneath
the comments – the comments! 'Ugly Cunt.' 'She ought to
fucking stay in a fucking rabbit suit.' 'I'd still fuck her. Cut a hole
in the rabbit suit and fuck her through the hole then throw her in
the river where she'd drown.' And then, as if to clarify – 'she'd
drown because the rabbit suit would become clogged with water
and it would be unmanageably heavy.' 'THIS IS NOT WHAT I
PAY MY TAXES FOR.' Nuts.

I didn't mind the rape threats, the violent stuff. I knew that was
bullshit. I'm not doing it down, obviously it's a rotten thing to
say, but I just had a hunch that if one of those undersized
rubbery mouth-breathers came round to mine and slithered in
through the catflap and tried to pistol-whip me round the face
with his flaccid penis then I'd be able to tell him where to get
off, yeah? No, the only comment which bothered me was a little
one-liner which said 'Chubbier than she thinks she is. Desperate
for attention. No one's ever going to love her.'

No one's ever going to love her. No one. Is Ever. Going. To.
Love. Her.

Harsh.

She has a swig of vodka.

I don't pay tax, actually. Never have. Well, the odd smidgen,
sheared off shit temp-job earnings during my fleeting attempts
to shimmy back into society. But I don't work. Don't earn.
Don't need to. (*Leans in, speaks in a deliberately loud whisper.*)
I've got a trust fund. (*Speaks normally again.*) Had a granny,
Dad's mum, died when I was six-ish. Left a big chunk of
money, half to me, half to my sister, so now I'm a bad-ass
motherfucker with an Assured Shorthold Tenancy on a studio
flat in Kensal Rise and all the wifi I can handle.

Swig of vodka.

I did try to get an actual real-world job, back then. The odd
interview. Silver-service waitress. Lettings assistant. Tube
driver. None of it stuck. I didn't know what I wanted to do.

Or rather, I probably actually did know what I wanted to do, but everything I thought I might want to do felt morally reprehensible. I know – 'poor little rich girl'. But fuck you, *fuck you*. Suffering's suffering. And after Dad, it felt – I felt – I mean, how can I trust myself? How can I trust anything *I* think when that's the mental stock I'm from? *I'm not good enough*. For *anything*. And also what kind of an evil selfish moron thinks such terrible things about someone with *mental-health issues* when mental health is such a *difficult, sensitive issue*? I deserve nothing. So I'll take what's given me. And what had been given me, via this fucking rabbit, was the internet.

So, to Google. If you don't need a job, you can spend a *lot* of life on Google.

Mental health

Mental-health difficulties

Mental-health forum

Child of mental-health-problem person

Mental health hereditary

Is it bad to like poetry by men

Philip Larkin T. S. Eliot patriarchy

Phillip Larkin T. S. Eliot racist

Moral rot

Thai Delivery Harlesden

Racism and sexism in poetry contagious to reader

Do I need to atone for liking male poets if I am a feminist

T. S. Eliot Wasteland

T. S. Eliot Wasteland breakdown

Suicidal

No social contact months

Samaritans

Years passing don't know how

Samaritans too ashamed to call

Samaritans was rude to them do I need to apologise

Twenties passing me by

X Factor can anyone audition

How often should I visit my family

Suicide

Used to be someone not someone any more

Googled suicide should I be worried

Dr Oetker pizza any nutrition

Lonely

Lonely

Search for meaning

Original death rabbit

Original death rabbit suicide

Original death rabbit her fault

Original death rabbit ugly cunt

Original death rabbit fat

Original death rabbit unloveable

'I said to my s– ' No.

You get the picture.

2008.

She pulls up a selfie from 2008 – she's aged quite a bit since 2006 and lost a bit of weight. Looks a bit louche, bit boozy.

Monday night, January. I'm having dinner with Penny. She's back from Yale, and she's softened a bit. She's got a boyfriend who's the second cousin of the second cousin of a Vanderbilt, she's chopped off her dreadlocks, and she's working at a magazine which *says* it's 'mainstream far left' but they do run ads for holidays in Tuscany on the website. Fact is – she's moving on. I am quite notably not. I'm quoting anonymous internet feedback given me two years previously.

'"No one's ever going to love her." I mean, I know that's just one comment on a stupid website about something which happened *years* ago, but I can't let it go, you know? I mean – what if they're right?'

I've been on this for a while.

'I think you need to stop dwelling on it.'

'But I *can't* – I mean, what if no one ever does love me?'

Friends – even Penny – take shit like this from me because I'm the victim of a trauma which they don't really understand, and because we're all twenty-four and we don't yet know that even people who've undergone terrible horrors and miseries and shocks should still be held to decent standards of behaviour, for their own sake if nothing else. Penny's braver than most in this regard. She sort of tells me when I'm being a dick.

'Maybe you should get a job.'

'I thought that jobs perpetuated systems of oppression.'

She dunks bruschetta in a little dish of olive oil.

'Not always.'

'I've kind of – look, now's not the time for a job. I'm running this not-for-profit' – when I said not-for-profit, by the way, that was a very deliberate choice of words. I was trying to impress the *old* Penny, even though she didn't seem to exist any more – 'this not-for-profit Richard Curtis Film Fan Forum which is basically full-time work, which is great, but it's making me feel double-sad about being by myself, you know? I don't even know what it is about being in love that really appeals to me. I mean – is it not being lonely? Or is it being rubber-stamped by society as someone who's good enough to be loved? Or is it just that love's *fun*, or perhaps I'm looking for someone to fill the – the – the – *love-void* which my mentally ill Dad could never fill – '

Penny can't take it any more.

'Okay. You need to stop. The Death Rabbit thing was two years ago.'

'Yeah but everything's forever on the internet – '

'That isn't really true.'

' – in people's eyes I'll always just be the Death Rabbit person – the cruel funeral-crasher who inspired twats to be twatty and who was fucking *crying* on her doorstep like a cunt when the paps came round – '

Penny interrupts me.

'So change it. It's your story. Change it.'

'What? *How?*'

'Write an article. Tell your side of it. Tell people the context. Tell them about your rabbit suit, tell them it was originally an ironic feminist rabbit suit. Tell them about the row with your sister. Tell them about your dad. Explain to them that you didn't plan it, you weren't in control of it, you hated it, and you regret it. Write it. Send it to me! You're a good writer. I'm ninety per cent sure we'll publish it.'

I wonder now if this was her way of saying sorry. Sorry for the self-righteous bullying, the student past, the 'let's stay self-loathing in the name of left-wing politics' pact that she'd broken.

I'm not blaming her for me. I get that this is all my fault.

Swig of vodka.

The very next day, I write it. I send it to Penny. She publishes it. Actual publishing in an actual magazine! I'm so proud. I really feel I've done the whole Death Rabbit episode justice, you know? Said all I had to say, so I can leave it behind. I think I've treated everyone involved fairly. Ish. You've got to twist some things for effect, haven't you? That's just part of being a journalist.

It gets quite the response. In the comments on the magazine website – 'Wow. Great story. Things are never quite what you think, are they?' 'She's so much prettier in real life.' 'It's so brave of her to speak up about her father's mental-health problems.

It's a really difficult issue.' One of my best friends from the Richard Curtis Film Fan Forum – duckface69 – twigs that I'm the Death Rabbit person and sends me a lovely message. Turns out he's a guy, too, and a jolly civil one at that. He calls me Anna, because that's my forum name. AnnaScott. 'Hi Anna, I hope to goodness I'm not overstepping any sort of mark here, but I admired your article so very much and I was wondering if perhaps you might be interested in joining me for some sort of beverage at a mutually convenient location at some point in the relatively near future? Yours, George (duckface69).' I say yes, absolutely. Where are you based? 'York.' Oh. Never mind. 'But I'm in London from time to time. Would you like to keep chatting on email until then?' Absolutely. I would. I absolutely would, George.

Someone suggests I join Twitter, which at this point is just this freaky little site which no one can quite see the point of. Mostly journalists. Bit weird.

I join.

My handle is @OriginalDeathRabbit, and I am an instant hit. I am followed and followed and followed. By midnight on the first day – the same day as the article comes out – my follower numbers are up in the thousands, even though all I've tweeted so far is the original Death Rabbit picture – the funeral one – and a jaunty 'Hear ye! Hear ye! Gosh. This is like being the town crier of my very own village. Haha.' I don't sleep that night. I just stay up refreshing and refreshing and refreshing Twitter and basking in the glow. Three browser windows open all night – the magazine website with the article on it, my Richard Curtis Film Fan Forum, and Twitter. All three all me. I feel godlike. Before I was internet-famous by chance, but now I'm back – on merit.

There's a moment, about four or five in the morning perhaps, when I look up from my screen and catch a glimpse of my reflection in my windowpane. Alone, in the dark, too wired on approval even to eat my Rustlers microwave burger, and I feel a vague sense that, well... is this what our grandfathers fought for?

Then one of the weathermen from ITV's *Daybreak* retweets me and I feel electric and I carry on until I fall asleep on the floor right by my desk, because I don't want to miss a minute.

I'm published. I'm a writer. Like *them*. What's left of my family will be so proud, I think. I've found my path!

A pause.

Next morning! Phone rings. Rare. It's my fucking *sister*. She stayed at home after Dad went nuts and moved in with Mum, then somehow mananged to get engaged to the man who worked in the Framlingham DVD rental shop, and now she's pregnant. FYI, I'm twenty-four, she's eighteen months younger than me and she's *pregnant*. Shouldn't that be on the news or something?

'What do you want?'

'Are you determined to destroy what remains of our family?'

She still steals all her lines from soap operas.

'What are you talking about?'

'Your article. How dare you? How *dare* you tell people about Dad? About us? About a *private conversation between you and me*? It's – I just – I just – '

I brace myself for the inevitable soapy gust.

'*I don't even know who you are any more!*'

I'm not having this. I. Am. Not. Having. This.

'You gave me permission! You said it was okay – '

'I said, you could write about your rabbit costume, and if absolutely necessary *allude vaguely to the fact that we were experiencing domestic stress*. You've written – okay, actually, right, I'll read you what you've written – "admittedly, I wasn't in great mental shape. But nor would you be if you'd just seen your much-loved father succumb to his demons and delicately slice through your cat's downy tawny ear as if he was opening a letter before setting upon you – " Seriously! I can't believe you – '

The UGLY CUNT *mimes holding the phone away from her ear.*

Meh-meh-meh. Actually when she first started speaking my stomach went through the floor, but now I've rationalised that she's just jealous. I'm a Twitter sensation and budding media superstar, and she's stuck back in Framlingham ineptly gestating a fetus. And it's not my fault she's decided that it's her responsibility to micro-manage the lives of our whole mental family like some sort of bleak-o pregnant Captain Mainwaring. I let her blather on for a bit, ranty-ranty-rant-rant and only find myself tuning back in when she says –

(*Acidic*.) 'Oh yes. And Suki Wilson called.'

I have a mouthful of toast on the go which makes me sound even more fabulously disrespectful.

'Who the fuck is Suki Wilson?'

'Jake Wilson's mother.'

I spat the toast onto my lap.

'Shit.'

'Mm-hm. She said, you should have called them. Warned them. Asked them. And – I'm paraphrasing here, I'm saying this much more nicely than she said it – she said you *really* shouldn't have described Jake's coffin as an Elvis coffin.'

I really shouldn't have. She was right. I absolutely should not have done that. The Wilsons had kind of forgiven me for the Original Death Rabbit thing, because I think they got that I hadn't meant to do anybody any harm et cetera, and when I'd first been outed I'd written to them and said sorry and stuff, but this time –

She shakes her head, takes a swig of vodka.

I punished myself. I lavishly internet-punished myself. I spent days, *weeks* – looking at pictures of women in bikinis on the internet. Women with washboard stomachs. That's my Achilles heel – I'm kind of wobbly-looking naked, kind of blancmange-oid, kind of stretch-marked, so I looked at photo after photo after photo to remind me how wrong I was, how disgusting I was compared to all these nice mainstream lingerie models. How I'd

never ever *ever be acceptable*. How I'd never be loved. Then
I thought I hadn't suffered enough so I moved on to porn – I'd
never watched porn before, I mean literally never. I once had a...
(*Hesitates, blushes a bit.*) once had a naughty mug where when
you poured the hot water in his trousers came off. But I'd never
seen real live professionals shagging. It was gross. Then after the
porn I moved on to escort review websites, where men review
hookers, and they say things like 'flat tits but does anal!' 'Bit of
a bitch.' 'Body off *Baywatch* face off *Crimewatch* LOL.' And
thought – I'd not get a good review as a hooker. I'd get one star at
best. I'd even fail at that. So I went on to plastic-surgery websites,
and worked out how much work I'd need done in order to look
more like 'Shiraz', the best-reviewed escort on the biggest escort
site, and how much it would eat into my savings. As if I were
costing a home-renovation project. Then I got scared and googled
'self-esteem', which led me to an article which said that in order
to love myself I must be tidy, for example organise my bras – and
then I went into a shame-spiral about not having enough bras to
merit organisation. So I went to the kitchen and sliced a tomato,
deliberately carelessly so the knife nicked my finger in a blissful
way, and drew blood. But of course it wasn't really self-harm,
because of the tomato. So no need to worry.

Then I went to bed, actual bed, and I tried to sleep but I couldn't,
so I tweeted. 'End of a blissful day reading wonderful responses
to my Hashtag Original Death Rabbit article, thank you all so
much! Hashtag blessed.'

Vodka.

2009! Ipswich Hospital. My sister's giving birth. Technically
I'm her birth partner – she's just split up with the Framlingham-
DVD-shop man, apparently he loved her very much but 'just
couldn't handle the whole dad thing' – so I'm hovering by the
vending machine with a knapsack full of Haribo and a two-litre
tub of Wet Wipes. I'm supposed to be in there cheerleading, but
I've had to excuse myself because ten minutes ago she went up
on all fours on the table and I swear I literally saw right up her
arsehole and it was the worst thing I've ever seen, so I offered
to go off and find more Fanta.

I'm checking Twitter. Twitter's going fabulously *fabulously* well for me. My Twitter account is basically The Ivy plus the Chiltern Firehouse plus the Chateau Marmont plus the greatest comedy club that's ever existed. I'm tweeting a broadsheet journalist lady who's at the centre of a glitzy, bitchy web of other sassy journo ladies. I tweet her most days and when she tweets back it's great, and when she doesn't it's kind of humiliating, but anyway I've just tweeted 'At sister's birth – she's a hero but MY GOD this is rough. Hashtag strength please.' And famous journo replied 'Darling how fabulous!' Then one of her chums chips in with 'Live-tweet birth?' And then a few more tweet 'yes! yes! yes! LOL' and I know I shouldn't really do this but for the first time in a while I've dipped below thirty thousand followers and… well. I knock on the door of the delivery room. Pop my head round.

'My love?'

She mimics her sister in labour.

NRRRGHGHGHGHGHGHGNNNNNGHAAAAAARRRGGHHH HHH!

'Hope it's going well. Was just wondering – how about if I live-tweet your birth? I think that would provide a really useful – um – service – '

GRAAAAAAGHHHHHHHHHGGHHHHHHHHH! UGH UGH UGH!

I take that as assent, and set to work. 'She's about a fist-worth dilated! I think she's going to poo on the table. Hashtag please don't poo on the table. Hashtag live birth.'

Pause.

I gained five thousand followers, and my sister stopped speaking to me. 'How would you feel if I posted a DESCRIPTION of your VULVA on a public noticeboard?' I'd be fine with it, I say. In fact – go on. Knock yourself out. I've removed my pants in readiness. She didn't get the joke – *quelle surprise* – and said: 'Is being famous on the internet really more important to you than what remains of your own family?' I explained to her that building my brand online was an important part of my job, my business, and

this was the way the world was going and she quite frankly
needed to shape up or ship out. Then she told me I was a
sociopath and hung up the phone.

Pause.

The worst thing about that whole live-tweet-birth thing, actually,
was that – well, the journos, the cool girls, hadn't meant it. 'Live-
tweet birth.' They said that as a joke, like it was the worst thing
anyone could possibly do under the circs. But I took them
seriously, I think because I was so giddy that they'd *all* tweeted
me at once, and went and did it. I – you know, I had my niggles,
but I couldn't really – (*Genuinely perplexed.*) I actually couldn't
really see why it was so wrong. And now the cool journo women
don't talk to me any more. One of them blocked me. I set up a
couple of new accounts so I could still follow them, and
sometimes I tweet them nice things – 'Great column today!
Major lols!' under assumed identities and I hope they'll reply, and
sometimes they do. But – yeah. That was – a bit of a bummer.

Swig of vodka.

And I'd got – yes, I'll use the word – a troll. But a *subtle* troll.
Went by the handle @hipsteripstercomedy. A quite Twitter-
famous British man, a clay sculptor and comedy writer, really
open about his problems with anxiety and depression and
massively sanctimonious about politics and witty about the
inanities of modern life, and how his family got him through,
and how all of us who suffer from mental-health issues need to
have compassion for one another and *stick together* blah blah
blah – which is easy to say when you've got a family to stick
together with. Not so much when you're –

She looks around at her empty flat.

Fungus the Bogeyman!

And maybe cos I was a teeny tiny bit dying of loneliness, I took
very strong exception to him. What he initially did to me – not
so bad. Just a link to a blog post about memes featuring real
people, and how 'damaged' those people tended to be by the
experience. Posted a link to my Twitter account, the implication
being that I was in some way 'damaged' by what had happened

to me, and that my 'pre-existing mental-health issues' might have been exacerbated by exposure to the public gaze.' I tweeted him – 'Thoughtful, interesting blog, love and light x' – then drank a bottle of vodka, set up an egg-troll Twitter, waited ten hours, and tweeted 'Get the fuck off the internet, mental-o – shouldn't you be weaving a basket somewhere to carry around your little bottle of thorazine?' 'Your comedy is shit.' 'Kill yourself.' 'Kill yourself.' 'Kill yourself.' Then I set up another egg account and tweeted some graphic rape threats to the feminist journalist ladies who blocked me, and then did the same to their husbands – who probably *loved* it – then I closed the computer and thought – that's the lowest I'll ever go. Never, ever, ever, ever again. I'm getting help. Tomorrow. I'll get help.

The mole popped up again that night. 'I said to my soul, I said to my soul – ' Ignored it. Some OCD bullshit. Fuck off.

My sister got back in touch with me three years later, in 2012. Olympics year!

She fiddles around on her computer and brings up a selfie from 2012 – she's in full Team GB souvenir-shop regalia and looks DISASTROUS.

She also pulls a vuvuzela out of the pocket of the rabbit suit and blows lustily on it.

I've had that ready and waiting this whole time. Worth it, I think?

She tucks the vuvuzela back in her pocket.

Twenty-twelve. It's Super Saturday in the stadium, and I'm a bit stressed. I've got Jessica Ennis and all that malarkey going on on television, three browsers open on my laptop and I'm trying to moderate a live *Notting Hill* watch-along with a bunch of rom-com-loving Olympics refuseniks on my iPad. I've almost run out of granny money, so I've got a JOB – YES A PAID JOB – now, writing copy for a wellness website. Eight hundred words on the 'is cashew butter the new almond butter', and Five Ways Clean Eating Will Enhance Your Meditation Practice. I've never physically met my employers, but I told them I was a yoga teacher and freelance business coach and they never bothered to check. I never have to leave the house, and the wage covers rent and precisely seven Iceland ready meals a week. I'm also trying to eat a microwave spaghetti and meatballs meal but rarely have a hand free long enough to do the business with the fork so every few minutes I just lower my face to the bowl and suck.

I don't go out. Once you don't go out for a while it gets hard to go out. I'm basically a tragic lonely elderly person except I'm twenty-seven.

To drown *that* out, I've become slightly Nazi on the Richard Curtis Film Fan Forum. For a while I allowed arguably healthy debate i.e. perhaps *Four Weddings and a Funeral* is structurally slightly stronger than *Notting Hill*, perhaps X plot-strand of *Love Actually* didn't quite do the others justice. But now I've completely flipped and I've decided that only VERY EXPLICITLY POSITIVE posts are permitted. I'm considering changing the forum name to the Richard Curtis Admiration-Only Film Fan Forum, but have yet to post this suggestion *in* the forum because I'm worried there'll be a big dramatic hoo-ha and things are a *tiny* bit delicate for me at the mo.

Then to top it all off, duckface69 keeps trying to meet up with me. We've been messaging on and off for three years, but he seems a cautious sort of fellow so he's only now inching towards making a firm sort of suggestion that it might be nice for the two of us to perhaps meet up for a pancake. I can't handle it. I mean – I'm up for love. If enduring, flawless romatic love were a guaranteed outcome of our meeting, then I'd be absolutely absolutely game for that. But without that guarantee, I am staying put. I ain't no fool.

Also, I'm not entirely clear what my sexual orientation is. I think – I mean, going back to the actual *people* I've spent time with back in the past and how that went? I think I'm probably bisexual. But I don't know how a person's supposed to figure that out. I imagine public figures naked, and then I feel so guilty and disgusted that I read LGBT activist blogs and they all seem massively morally superior to me and it seems exhausting and I'm not sure I can hack it. I dunno. Love's just... bleurgh. People are so weird. Why bother?

I message him.

'I just don't know if I'm quite ready to take our relationship to that level.' And a 'winking' emoticon which I immediately worry is far too saucy.

He sent a really sweet reply. He always does. He's a really really sweet guy. So so so so so so *so so* sweet.

'Well, you know, if is doesn't go well then perhaps we can just do an *About Time* on it?! Zoom back and do it all over again! LOL.'

I'm about to suggest we just have cybersex instead – IM cybersex, so you can do it while for example eating or clipping fingernails – when I get a call.

I close the discussion and pick up the Skype.

'Hello?'

She's angry. Three years have elapsed since we last spoke, and she's somehow managed to maintain the exact same pitch of wounded rage.

'Why the fuck have you got sauce on your face?'

I look in the mirror. I do have sauce on my face. A muzzle of sauce. My reply is cool. Chilly, even. I may have a muzzle of sauce, I think, but *I still have my dignity.*

'I've been eating meatballs.'

'Okay.' She attempts small talk. 'So. Great about Jessica Ennis, huh?'

I look at the telly, now on mute. Medal ceremony.

'Yes. No. That's... brilliant. Good for her.'

'Yeah yeah great.'

'Okay, so I've got some news.'

'Mm-hm.'

'Well, two bit of news, actually. Good news and bad. First, I'm getting remarried!'

'Yayness!'

'Also, there's been a change in Dad's circumstances.'

My middle goes hollow. I've been doing a great, awful, self-hating job of ignoring the escalating mad-dad situation.

'Okay… what's happening?'

'His therapy group's being discontinued. A cuts thing. And he's really not improved at all lately so we think that it might be time to look into a stint of private residential care.'

'Great. Can I – uh – do anything?'

She light another cigarette.

She wanted *money*. A significant, three-weeks-in-Majorca-style sum of money from my Granny fund. She didn't twig that I'd spent the last seven years living almost entirely off my Granny fund apart from the wellness writing, because I'd kind of sort of told her that I earned money from my online work. Might have given her the impression that the Film Fan Site and the Death Rabbit Twitter and my 'journalism' brought in slightly more income than they actually did, which is to say none at all.

I say something like 'But aren't we actually *hurting* him by giving him money? Don't we have to leave him alone to reach his rock bottom?'

'No, that's alcoholics. Schizophrenics you can give money to.'

'Oh.'

I don't tell her I've not got the money any more. In an attempt to stall I agree to make my first visit back home for years, to attend a support group for families of people suffering severe mental illnesses. My sister's been going for a few months, which I think explains her willingness to ask me for help, and her slightly reduced level of narky shoutiness.

And there's something else going on. I seem to have not-quite-stopped posting on the egg-troll accounts, the abusive ones. I've actually got good at it. Open one up, close it when someone threatens to call the police, open a new one. I've rationalised it by saying 'Well, I'm doing good in the world with the Richard

Curtis Film Fan Forum and wellness copywriting, so it's okay if I put some bad into the world as well?' And I've focused all the bad on @hipsteripster comedy who FUCKING DESERVES IT.

We're locked in a weird war, me and him – I troll him, he writes a long, windy blog about life as a mentally ill troll victim. I respond with more trolling. He repeats. Sometimes the *Guardian* gets involved and prints one of his little whinges. Publishes a picture of him looking sad with some Diazepam and a laptop and his kids in the background.

I tell myself that he's an 'old white man' so it's okay, and I know that's not true. Then I tell myself that he's a 'privileged mentally ill person', in that he has people who love him and I don't and my dad doesn't, and I sort of believe that's true, even though I know in my heart that it's not. And I hate him because he talks about his 'mental illness' like it's the worst thing in the world, but he's got fucking *anxiety*, and people who love him and help him with it – and he has no fucking idea how lucky he is! He doesn't fucking understand! He's so fucking privileged! He's the worst one in his family which means he gets to fucking *talk* about it!

Pause.

Sometimes I think I don't use the word 'privilege' right.

Pause.

Back to it. I know I'm not well. But I'm in so deep by this point that I can't get out. The shame. One night I get up and brave the outside, and walk and walk and walk until I reach a main road, and I dart across the main road and sit in the little bit of grass between the lanes, and hug the intersection and watch the lorries swoosh by, pre-dawn, for hours, and I think 'Be brave enough to run. Dart across, like a cat. They're big, the lorries. Just a little bump to them, and you won't have to try any more. Be brave enough. Be brave enough. Be brave enough.'

'I said to my soul, I said to my soul – ' NO. Be brave enough.

Then I remember that the author Cheryl Strayed who wrote *Wild* which was a film with Reese Witherspoon in wrote a book called *Brave Enough*, and I briefly mentally inventory Cheryl

Strayed's achievements and relationship life and compare them to my own, and I press my face into the grass and taste the dirt and *scream* at myself, at life, at my mind at it all – at *how come these people get to exist and do things when I don't?*

And I think 'wow'. If anyone knew what I was up to right now, they'd think I was completely mad.

I have dirt in my mouth, which I spit back onto the grass. I've not had water for a day, my spit's like glue. Be brave enough.

Pause.

I'm not brave enough. I wait for dawn, for a gap in the traffic, dart across to the verge and walk to a twenty-four-hour McDonald's where I order three Diet Cokes and a Big Breakfast, which was a treat when I was little – Big Breakfast! Day out! Flume park! – and for a moment I think I see Dad's face in the sausage patty, and I start to cry. Then I look around and see – not even kidding – THREE other people sitting alone staring at McDonald's breakfasts at dawn, all looking miserably at their phone screens, and I wonder if I should pass round a note suggesting we all get together for Christmas.

Then I go home and write an advertorial for a smoothie maker, paint one fingernail and Instagram it. Hashtag hot pink hashtag Fridays hashtag yay!

Still. To be clear – *I'm* not the mad one in my family.

She drinks some vodka.

The Familes of Those with Mental-Health Difficulties Support Group is held – weirdly – in the gym of a local prep school. It smells of crash mats and plimsolls, and there are big thick climbing ropes which make my mind flick uncontrollably back and forth between images of pirates and suicide. Me, my sister and the nearest and dearest of various local nutjobs sit in a circle while a woman called Patricia facilitates what she calls 'the thorny conversations, the unsayable which really must be said.' My sister is reading out her homework, a list of 'Real-Deal Affirmations' about my father.

'My dad did not hurt the cat because he didn't love us.'

'My dad did not hurt the cat because he didn't love the cat.'

'My dad hurt the cat because he was suffering from an illness. An illness like any other, an illness like the flu, or like a headache, or like gastric flu.'

She gets a round of applause which I don't think her effort warrants. Patricia moves on, to a section of the session where we address the importance of self-care. 'It can be tempting to use unhealthy distractions to help dull the pain of our situation, or even to help us avoid it altogether. Does anyone here think they might be doing that?

My sister's left hand shoots up in the air, her right hand points at me.

'She does! My sister. I think she lives a fantasy life on the internet to avoid having to deal with our reality.'

I'm about to chime in with a hearty and fully warranted 'How DARE you?!' when Patricia saves me. 'If we'd all like to keep the focus on ourselves – '

I excuse myself to go to the toilet and tweet from my Original Death Rabbit account – 'At support group for families of people with mental-health difficulties. Hashtag tough hashtag facing up to stuff hashtag challenging' then sit and stare at the back of the cubicle door. Someone's written 'Mrs Clayton cupped my balls!' on it. I root around in my handbag, find a biro and for no good reason I write underneath 'Was it while she was sucking you off?' And I marvel at the sheer physical solidity of my work and for a moment I think 'will that be my legacy? Is that what'll survive of me? When all the internet's floated off to wherever-the-fuck, will I wish I'd scrawled it all on a toilet door instead?

I check Twitter. My tweet's been retweeted fifteen times, a couple of people have written 'awwwwww BABE good luck xxx', and one person – oh, look it's @hipsteripstercomedy – has written 'any other MH folks' – that means, 'people with mental-health difficulties', and he's using 'folks' so as not to exlude the transgender and non-binary communities – 'feel a little uncomfy with @OriginalDeathRabbit using her MH family member to garner sympathy/follows? Love and light, of course, but hmm…'

And a SEA MONSTER rears up inside me, and I'm just about to log in to my egg-troll account to dish out some justice when my sister comes in and bangs on the door and says – 'We have to go! Come on! If you're not too chicken to come out and *actually face up to life* – ' and in my fury I draft the savagest tweet ever to @hipsteripstercomedy, a tweet which somehow manages to distil the distinctive tone, phraseology, and linguistic hallmarks of all the previous trolling into one detailed, violent incitement to suicide *including a suggested method and details of where to obtain materials*, and I send it. And I realise, a moment too late – that I've sent it from my Original Death Rabbit account. I have unveiled myself.

She drinks vodka.

Forty-five minutes later, and my sister and I are in the car park of the private psychiatric hospital. My father's there – there's a payment-plan thing so they don't need my money right now – and my sister thinks I should go in and see him. I disagree. I can't go in. I have to go to Oxford.

'Why do you have to go to Oxford?'

'I have a date.'

'A date?'

Oxford's halfway between London and York, that's where me and DuckFace69 are meeting.

'Yeah. You're allowed to get married all the time, so I'm allowed a date, right? It just isn't a convenient time for me to visit Dad.'

'But you're *here*. You're two hundred feet away from him. If you want to visit him literally all you have to do is turn forty-five degrees to your left and walk ten paces.'

'No. Sorry.'

'Are you scared? There's nothing to be scared of, you know. He's ill, but he's still Dad.'

'Yeah – I know, but. Sorry.'

I turn and walk away, get into the car, and drive. To Oxford. Where there'll be love. Connection. An actual human who isn't a tweet or a handle or a Skype call or a film or a meme or TV. A human who'll touch me, and I'll touch them back and healing will begin.

'I said to my soul – '

Perhaps this is my moment, I think. Perhaps this is the last time I'll not have anything true to Instagram on Bank Holiday weekends – perhaps I'll meet him and then on Twitter I'll be all like 'YAAAAY! SQUEEEEE! Heart emoji heart emoji heart emoji.'

If I'm not in prison.

I accelerate, too fast for the drive of the mental hospital.

My sister runs along behind me shouting 'Hey! Come back! *That's my car!*'

Pause.

I was scared. I was. But not because of Dad. I was scared of the psychiatric hospital because –

I saw something.

Three days ago. Stone-cold sober.

I saw –

I saw –

I was looking at the door. At the doorknob.

And just once –

I saw –

I saw Aladdin running across the doorknob. A tiny little Aladdin. Not exactly the Aladdin from the Disney film. But very similar.

If your father is in a psychiatric hospital and you see Aladdin running across the doorknob and you have a bit of an addictive internet issue, then whatever you do *do not* google 'psychosis'. Okay?

Mental health is a really difficult issue.

She finishes the vodka.

Oxford! Two hours later. Oxford in November is freezing but wonderful, beautiful, the most romantic place in the world! Clear night, snap in the air, the whole city *iced* like a bun. Duckface69 met me in Radcliffe Square. 'I – I – I thought it might be fun if we met exactly in front of the main entrance of the Radcliffe Camera, positioned centrally in the doorway, as it's a perfect arch which I always thought would provide a wonderful setting for a couple to meet.' I think he may watch too many romantic comedies.

We've been on our date for an hour, and it's going reasonably well considering he's the first stranger I've spent this long with since – fuck knows. I'm distracted – @hipsteripstercomedy hasn't posted since my trolling, and I just *know* there's something wrong – but I'm trying to focus on my date. He's a chubby man in his mid-thirties, a secondary-school English teacher, with a shock of curly ginger hair. He's wearing a worn-looking harlequin-patterned wooly jumper and cords. We're in the pub. So far we've only talked about Richard Curtis films, and only in the most positive terms, but now we're branching out. He's talking about his own romantic aspirations.

'I mean – I'd very much enjoy falling in love I think – I've felt affection for – individuals of the opposite sex, but – my dear, you seem distracted.'

I am distracted. I am.

'It's just – I'm – ' And I let rip. I say it. Like Patricia told me to. I say the unsayable. 'I'm beginning to – to – lose faith. I'm beginning to think that maybe love isn't all around us. That maybe there is *something* all around us – but it's not love. It's something else.'

He looks genuinely baffled.

'What, like... Christmas?'

'I'm just sad. That's all. Just a bit down lately.'

He leans across the table, takes my hand in mine, looks me in the eye, and speaks. Slow, steady, reassuring, strong.

'Whenever I get gloomy with the state of the world, I think about the arrivals gate at Heathrow Airport. General opinion's starting to make out that we live in a world of hatred and greed, but I don't see that. It seems to me that love is everywhere. Often it's not particularly dignified or newsworthy, but it's always there – fathers and sons, mothers and daughters, husbands and wives, boyfriends, girlfriends, old friends. When the planes hit the Twin Towers, as far as I know none of the phone calls from the people on board were messages of hate or revenge – they were all messages of love. If you look for it, I've got a sneaky feeling you'll find that love actually is all around.'

I've heard that before, I say. I've definitely heard that somewhere before.

'*Love Actually*, silly! Silly billy. It's Hugh Grant's monologue at the beginning.'

He picks up my hand and kisses it and says. 'Come on, admit it. It's cheered you up, hasn't it? I've cheered you up. I always cheer you up when you're having a bad day. Because I'm your one. The one. And you are my Anna Scott.'

I excuse myself to go to the ladies, leave the pub via the back entrance, and drive my sister's car home. I check Twitter in traffic – there's been a drama. Several hours ago, it seems, @hipsteripstercomedy passed away, according to his girlfriend, who's commandeered his Twitter account. He took his own life after a long struggle with severe depression, compounded – she says – by being the victim of an internet troll.

Lights another cigarette.

(*Slowly.*) Mental health is a really difficult issue.

That was thirty-six hours ago. I don't know how you're supposed to feel after you do something like this to someone. I feel – it's like when I took the school hamster home and lost it I suppose, times a million. Or when you accidentally shut a door in someone's face. Or – no. There isn't a thing. It's – pfft. I don't know. Nothing.

But I wanted to make this thing, this video to tell you what's gone on, to let you know that whatever you think, there's always a story. That hate doesn't grow in a vaccum. That there's fifteen different sides to everything, and it's all always complicated. I was going to make a big speech. But now I get here and it's – nothing. I've got nothing.

Pause.

One of the symptoms of schizophrenia – because I was looking this up too, all this time, I *did* care – is that all your thoughts sort of fall out of your head. You grasp for one, and it's not there. It's gone. I get what that's like now, it's happened with my feelings.

Some people would say it's shock. But I don't think it is. I think it's Life – God – numbing me out enough that I'm able to do what I need to do, like when ISIS people give people drugs before they put them in a cage and burn them.

She strokes the bunny suit, and clicks her cigarette lighter.

Equal parts polyester, rayon and acrylic, untreated, not flame retardant.

Pause. She looks thoughtful.

I wonder if that's what all of this has been about – this last – whole – God – decade. I've been trying to replicate Dad's illness, in whatever ways I could, to get close to him. I took my functioning mind – which is the real privilege, isn't it? A brain which works even a bit? – and plugged it into – (*Indicates the laptop.*) this endless demonic mosaic of other people's stupid bullshit words words words, egos fighting egos like kamikaze pilots in the sky – until it broke. My heart broke, then my spirit, then my morals, then my mind – and then I broke someone else in turn, and now he's dead, and soon I will be too.

Thank you, Tim Berners Lee. Thank you, thank you, thank you. I bow down to you the way a dying alcoholic bows down to whoever the fuck first left grapes in a bottle too long.

'Man hands on misery to man,
It deepens like a coastal shelf.'

A half-smile.

I've heard that somewhere before. Naughty Philip Larkin. My forbidden long-lost love.

Here's another one. 'Mr Bleaney':

'The dread
That how we live measures our own nature,
And at his age having no more to show
Than one hired box should make him pretty sure
He warranted no better, I don't know.'

Her face crumples at this. She wipes away a tear.

It's nice, my flat, isn't it? I sometimes think that. It could have been nice. It has period features.

It would have been my birthday tomorrow. Thirty-two. So still technically a millennial. My sister sent me this cake.

She gets up, goes to the sideboard, and pulls out a birthday cake with a candle on it. Puts it on the sideboard. Lights the candle on the top of it.

And a card which says, 'I know it's awful, but I love you.'

She loves me. Someone does love me.

I loved things once.

I wish I didn't have to do this.

A beat. She's angry, suddenly. Furious, breathless, maybe sobbing – or on the verge of it.

You know 'An Arundel Tomb'? What will survive of us is love? That's bullshit now. Bullshit. Because what will survive of so many of us way-too-permeable, fragile, once-hopeful, precious, lonely, furious, trapped, addicted people who could have been better – appalled souls caged in hunched clenched bodies and brutalised by broken minds – minds made up of jabs and snippets and other people's fifth-hand quasi-political pseudo-morals and *opinions* and *junk* is *not* love. It's bile. It's self-righteous pointlessly crusading bitty formless wordy bile, lowering, pointless incessant *viewpoints* –

She sits down in front of the computer. Opens a browser window. Stops dead. Reads, astonished.

'Twitter star @hipsteripstercomedy "back from the dead" after suicide hoax to highlight the dangers of online trolling. "People *need to know* that their words online have consequences, and if I gave a troll a scare, then great. I'm not sorry."'

She stops reading.

Well I never. Motherfucker.

She starts typing. Stops. Sits for a moment, winded.

I said to my soul.

Gets up. Goes urgently over to the little bookshelf. Pulls out a volume of T. S. Eliot poetry. Sits back at her laptop. Urgently leafs through the book, looking for a specific poem. Reads it.

Yeah.

Pause. She reads. Nods.

Yeah.

She turns back to the webcam.

'I said to my soul, be still and wait without hope, for hope would be for the wrong thing; wait without love, for love would be love of the wrong thing; there is yet faith, but the faith and the love are all in the waiting. Wait without thought, for you are not yet ready for thought; So the darkness shall be the light, and the stillness the dancing.'

She closes her laptop. Takes off her bunny suit – underneath, she's wearing shorts and T-shirt.

She looks quite childlike. Fragile. This should be a bit shocking.

Thirty-two is young. You can start again at thirty-two.

She blows out the candle. She sits in the stillness with the book on her lap.

End.

A Nick Hern Book

Original Death Rabbit first published in Great Britain in 2019 as a paperback original by Nick Hern Books Limited, The Glasshouse, 49a Goldhawk Road, London W12 8QP, in association with Jermyn Street Theatre, London

Original Death Rabbit copyright © 2019 Rose Heiney

Rose Heiney has asserted her moral right to be identified as the author of this work

Extracts from 'An Arundel Tomb', 'This Be the Verse'and 'Mr Bleaney' by Philip Larkin reprinted with the permission of The Estate of Philip Larkin, published by Faber & Faber Ltd

Extract from 'East Coker' by T.S. Eliot reprinted with the permission of The Estate of T.S. Eliot, published by Faber & Faber Ltd

Extract from *Love Actually* reprinted with kind permission of Richard Curtis

Cover photograph by Will Herman

Designed and typeset by Nick Hern Books, London
Printed in the UK by Mimeo Ltd, Huntingdon, Cambridgeshire PE29 6XX

A CIP catalogue record for this book is available from the British Library

ISBN 978 1 84842 829 4